Uncommon Prayers
for Couples

Conception Prayers
for Couples

Uncommon Prayers for Couples

Daniel R. Seagren

BAKER BOOK HOUSE
Grand Rapids, Michigan

Copyright 1980 by
Baker Book House Company
ISBN: 0-8010-8173-4

Printed in the United States of America

PREFACE

This is not a marriage manual. In fact, it isn't even a prayer book. More than that, these prayers are hardly uncommon.

Having said this, what makes them **uncommon** is that many if not most of these prayers are never put into words. That is one of the marvelous aspects of prayer: prayers don't always need words. A sigh, a tear, a sob or a shout often do as well as words.

Even so, there comes a time when prayers must be put into words. That's what happens here.

Marriage is a marvelous invention. Actually, it was God's idea in the first place and nothing has come along to improve upon it. Read these outbursts of ecstasy and rejoice with them; read these agonizing sobs and weep. Turn the searchlight on your soul and let the heat and light heal your hurts. Marriage can be fragile but it can be tough, too!

In our culture courtship is important, extremely important. The same is true of the honeymoon (as you'll discover when you read these prayers). Marriage can be an exquisite affair. It can also evolve into a drab existence or even a nightmare. Estrangement is no stranger to marriage, although we hope and pray that these two will never meet. If they do, there's always hope of reconciliation.

These prayers are no respecters of age or gender. The agonies and ecstasies of **courtship, marriage, parenting, estrangement** and reconciliation are verbalized even when verbalizing is difficult or seemingly impossible. It is hoped that these uncommon prayers will touch your life and that of someone you love.

Read what you see and read between the lines. As you get involved, why not talk to the Lord in your own style? He's anxious to communicate and He might even surprise you with His infinite wisdom and understanding. **So be it, Lord.**

CONTENTS

ESTRANGEMENT 69

Because people are human, and because the world can be a rather troublesome place, and because marriage is always vulnerable to attack, disappointments and disillusionments do occur. Here you will hear some broken hearts crying for help, and you will see how complicated life can be.

RECONCILIATION 85

There is reason to rejoice when two estranged individuals reconcile their differences and forgive one another. Some couples quarrel merely because of the joy of making up, but this is certainly not a good practice. Marriage is too fragile to fool with, in spite of the fact that marriage can be extremely rugged. When given half a chance, reconciliation is usually a far better alternative than continued estrangement.

AN ANNOTATED BIBLIOGRAPHY 99

COURTSHIP

The Long Road Ahead

Lord,
when I was much younger
we sang a song in Sunday School
which went like this:
> The road may be long
> but my Savior is strong...
Remember?

You probably remember
how we changed the words:
> The road may be rough
> but my Savior is tough...

Maybe this isn't such bad theology.

When I think of marriage
I think of it as a journey
to some far away place...

I think of it as a leap
into the unknown...

I think of it as an
exotic adventure...

> I'm excited, Lord.

I wait breathlessly for the phone to ring
I wait anxiously for the smile on his face

I fuss endlessly to make sure I'm fit to be seen
   Then I take my eyes off him
   and as I look around I
   am afraid . . .

      Am I worthy?
      Does he love me?
      Can our love endure?

      Then I scold myself
      for taking my eyes off him.

And then I scold myself for
taking my eyes off You.

Lord, go with us
each step of the way. We need Someone
who is both **strong** and **tough**!

Thought He'd Never Ask

Lord, I thought he'd never ask.
I did everything reasonable
except ask him myself.

   Tonight I heard those wonderful words:
   "Will you marry me?"
   Will you marry me?

Four words—fourteen letters!!!
They will change my life
   completely
   irrevocably
   eternally.

For thirty-eight months
I've waited
   dreamed

schemed
prayed
and now that he's mine
I couldn't even answer him.

A million times, Lord,
I had rehearsed this moment
but what did I do?

I wept like a baby
I shook like a leaf.
I'm so embarrassed
I could die
but never have I wanted to live
more than just now.

Thanks, Lord,
for waiting with me.

Engaged or Disengaged?

Is it really true, Lord,
that long engagements
are as bad as short ones?

We're engaged.
We want to get married.
I want to get married NOW!
He wants to wait a year.

What should we do, Lord?

He wants to finish school
but I'm sick of my job.

He wants us to save a little money
but I could live on love.

He wants to please his parents (and mine)
but who cares what they think?

We're not engaged, Lord.
We're disengaged.

I'm taken out of circulation
while he solves silly equations.

How can I know what he's doing until midnight?
I could spy on him but I won't.

Um, ah, could it be, Lord, that our
engagement is a cooling-off period
rather than a warmup? Before he asked me
things were getting pretty hot. We could have
been burned pretty easily now that I
look back on it.

Lord, I'll wait.
I think I can manage it.
But I don't want to be engaged
(or disengaged) too long.

Maybe a year is about right.

The Myth of Incompatibility

You know how sure I was
that You brought us together.
Now I'm not so sure . . .

   I'm timid—he's bold
   I'm tall—he's short
   I'm slim—he's stout
   I'm affluent—he's not

I like coffee—he likes tea
I'm fond of art—he hates it
I'm crazy about flowers—he's allergic

I prefer to fly—he'd rather drive

14

I like cross-country—he prefers downhill

My folks are a bit stiff
He says they're snobs

His folks are a bit retiring
He says they're backward

My parents are religious
His are devout

I'm sanguine—he's choleric . . .

Why am I saying this?
You know better than I

What shall we do, Lord?
I want to marry him
He wants to marry me

My parents say, "Wait."
His respond, "Go ahead."

Mine ask, "Why?"
His reply, "Why not?"

Lord, is it true that in Christ
incompatibility is a myth?

Do all things work together
for those who love God—
and each other?

On Second Thought...

I spotted her in the balcony
from where I sat in the choir.
It was love at ninety-nine feet.

Eagerly I awaited the sermon's end
in order to push through the crowd

to intercept her before
she got away.

Up close she didn't look quite the same.

She was taller than I thought.
Her skin wasn't as smooth as
I had imagined and when she
smiled I noticed how crooked
her teeth were.

I hastily retreated
without saying a word.
My heart sank as
my hopes vanished.

She came back again. And again.
From my secure vantage point
I watched from a distance.

Then she disappeared as silently
as she had appeared.

I never knew her name.
I never bothered to find out
but now I can't get her
out of my mind.

Please, Lord,
if You wouldn't mind,
could you bring her back again?
Only one more time?

Trapped!

Good Lord, what have we done?
She's sweet and pretty

as a rosebud
but innocent she's not.

> We played it cool for quite awhile
> until we began to tire of one another.

I should have known better, Lord.
I know it is dangerous
to play with fire
but I thought
I could handle it.

> Every night the guys would taunt
> Every night she would tease
> Every night I vowed to make it the last
> but I never did.

> Then it happened.
> It just happened.
> That's all.

Unplanned
Unprepared
Unrehearsed
Unfulfilling

I don't hate her, Lord,
but I don't love her, either.
In fact, I don't even like her.

> But now
> I'm obligated.

Ultimatums
are awful foundations
on which to build
a marriage,
aren't they?

You're Not Meant for Each Other

That's all I ever hear, Lord:

"Don't marry."
"You'll be sorry."
"Life is too short."
"You're not meant for each other."
"Don't be a fool."

The more I listen
the worse it gets.

We need each other, Lord.
We are meant for each other.
We were brought together
for a purpose.

Why can't people mind their own business?
Why must everyone meddle in our affairs?
Why would our own parents turn against us?

Lord, we're not rebellious
nor are we stupid or naive!

We will have difficulties.
We will have some rough adjustments.
We undoubtedly will feel sorry
for ourselves now and then.

But we'll make it, Lord.
I know we will.

What hurts so much
is not our friends
failing to understand
but the blindness of our relatives.

Lord,
how can I convince my people

that I want to marry a person,
not a wheelchair?

Nightmare on Cloud Nine

Only a short time ago
I was living on Cloud Nine
but I'm not living there anymore, Lord.

We liked each other
and thought it would
be exciting to live together
to see if we were
compatible or not.

Now we'll never know.

It worked beautifully for awhile.

It was like playing house.
It was devilishly romantic.
It was so intimate, so seductive . . .

But then
I started feeling guilty
(I wasn't brought up this way).

She began to get possessive
(she thought she might lose me).

I resented her nagging and
she resented my resistance.

I was trapped, Lord,
and I didn't like it
so we split.

No, I didn't move out.
We still share the rent
but not much else.

Lord, I wasn't listening
awhile ago
but now I rather suspect
that You
had a better idea.

Two-Way Chauvinism

We believe in equal rights:
    equal pay for equal jobs
    emancipation from slavery
    elimination of prejudice . . .

In fact, Lord, we agree
that Adam and Eve share equally
in the blame which has alienated spouses
everywhere.

We have been engaged for over a year
and we have good paying jobs but
    we cannot agree on the
    division of our income.

    We plan to marry when we have
    saved enough for a hefty
    downpayment on the
    home of our dreams.

Here's our problem, Lord:
    the downpayment must be my money—
    the payments must come from my income
which may be quite logical except
    she insists that
    her money is
    her money.

Her concept is simple:

we'll live off my income
and save hers—in her name.
When I bring up the matter
she counters with an epithet
of **male chauvinism** . . .
One of these days I suppose
I'll counter with charges of
female chauvinism.

> Lord, just what did You mean
> that two shall become one?

I Do, I Do, I Do!

Why would he want me, Lord?
I'm lonely but not desperate.
I'm willing but hardly eager.
What could be causing him
to consider risking his life
for a widow with three little ones
hanging on her neck?

> Is it love?
> > pity?
> > altruism?
> > duty?
> Oh, if I only knew . . .

Forgive me, Lord,
for thinking such thoughts.

He loves me—
I know he does!
Or, does he love my little ones
more than he loves me? Or less?

Why should I think thoughts like this, Lord?

What makes me hesitate?

Is it fear?
pride?
memories?
selfishness?
Or, am I just stubborn???

Should I be concerned
whether he loves my little ones
as much as he loves me?
Does it matter?

Lord, I want to say yes,
I do, I do, I do
but I've got to be sure
not only for my sake
but theirs . . .
and Yours!

Never Too Late

Lord, I'm getting so old . . .
Will I ever get married?
Will anyone want me?
Is it wrong
to want to stay single?
Is it right
to marry just for the sake
of getting married?

I don't think I've been in love.
I don't think I've met the right one.

Why should I marry?
Why should I worry?
But I do!

Did You create us all
with a built-in
yearning to share our lives
with someone we love?
Are we abnormal if we never cross
the threshold of marital bliss?

Why do people
think it strange
when thirty
comes and goes
but marriage
is not in sight?

Sure, Lord, it's lonely
at times
but I'd much rather
be unhappily single
than unhappily married
even though personally
I'm not unhappy—only unmarried.

Wine, Women, and Song

Lord, if I had
only become a
Christian sooner!
I know You forgive
and I'm told You forget.
But I can't!

Too many women have crossed my path.
Too many times I tripped them up.
Lord, there's got to be a limit somewhere.

I don't think I could marry—

I don't think I should, either.

I was a beast, Lord,
with only one thing in mind—
  wine
  women
  and, well, Lord,
  I'm not sure about the song.

Those days are behind me.
Their desire has been taken away
  but now **she** has
  entered my life.

I didn't plan it, Lord.
She just happened by
and I don't know what to do.
  Can I be gentle and kind?
  Can I start over again?
  Should she know of my past
  or is it wiser to show her
  who I am rather than
  who I was?

Lord, I can't hurt this child—
She's Yours and so am I
but I'm not sure I can trust myself—
yet I'll never know until I try.

  Whatever happens, Lord,
  I'm Yours to command.

I Can But I Won't!

Lord, I've told him
over and over

that I won't marry him
but he keeps asking.
  What should I do next?
Lord, I can give You
ten good reasons why I
won't even date him now:

> He doesn't believe in You
> He won't go to church with me
> He speaks ill of his family
> His language is often unpleasant
> His money doesn't impress me
> His manners are uncouth
> His attitude is irresponsible
> His reputation isn't worth a dime
> His friends are fair-weather acquaintances
> He doesn't deserve a Christian wife!!!

Why is it, Lord, he won't
take "No!" for an answer?
Is it because
> he can't find a decent girl in his crowd?
> he's trying to prove something?
> I have standards he unconsciously respects?
> You once got through to him?

Years ago he was a fine Christian
but somewhere he took the wrong fork
in the road.

I guess I make him sound more arrogant
than he actually is but he's
not fooling anyone with
his smooth talk
and I'd be a fool to think he'd change
after I marry him which I won't.

Sorry, Lord, I may be out of breath
but I'm not out of my mind.
Just thought You'd like to know!

She's Everything I Don't Want

Lord, she's everything
I don't want but
I keep going back for more.

   She's fickle (I know
   I could never trust her)

   She's beautiful (but its
   her pride and joy)

   She's talented (except none
   of it is reserved for You)

   She's liberated (she would
   never consider me an equal)

   She's ruthless (everything
   must go her way)

I guess, Lord, I enjoy
being seen with her
more than I enjoy
being with her.

   That is stupid
      idiotic
      or perhaps sardonic . . .

Whatever, Lord, she'll make a poor wife
and undoubtedly an even worse mother.
Even so I can't say no.

   Forgive me, Lord.
   In spite of my

26

better judgment
I plan on marrying her.

If only I had the strength
to send her on her merry way
but I don't.

Just one thing, though.
If it doesn't work out,
I'll blame myself,
not You.

Get Me to the Church on Time

Ever since I was a little girl
I've dreamed of a church wedding.
Now, Lord, I'm not so sure.
In fact, I'm confused.
He doesn't want to get married at all!

If we do marry, he says
he can't handle a church affair:
"Too much politicking among relatives."
"That gift business is a racket."
"Everybody has their palms out:
organist
preacher
custodian
florist . . ."
And, in a way, he's right!

It seems such an unnecessary expense
when ninety seconds in a courthouse
will do just as well.
Or will it?

Marriage is sacred, isn't it?

27

It's almost a sacrament, isn't it?
You actually solemnize the vows, don't You?
   "Whom God has joined together
   let no man put asunder."
Lord, what a way to begin life together.
Maybe we need more time . . .
Maybe we're not meant for each other.

   With Your help I'll do it!
   I'll get to the church on time
   but I won't show up at the courthouse.
   I might lose him, Lord, because
   I can't afford to lose You.

MARRIAGE

Nuptial Neurosis (Hers)

In a few moments, Lord,
I'll walk down the aisle
to say "I do" in a voice
choked with emotion.
> I want to run away, Lord!
> No, I'm not terribly nervous—
> I'm afraid.

He looks so tall standing there—
> and strong
> and handsome
but I suppose all grooms are like that.

What if I can't love him?
What if I can't give him a child?
What if I can't make him happy?

> Will he still love me?
> Will he be patient and kind?
> Will he want to make me happy?

Why didn't I think about this
before I got this far?

> My father's arm is reassuring
> and his handkerchief has dried my tears
> but they'll come again
> and he'll be gone.

31

Help me, Lord
  I'm worried about tripping
  on my gown
  but that's not my real concern
  although I wish it were . . .

Oh, that's the Bridal Suite
It's too late now, Lord.
  Please, take my other arm
  and promise You'll never let go.
  Promise?

Nuptial Neurosis (His)

I can see her, Lord,
waiting on her father's arm.
She looks beautiful,
more beautiful than I
imagined.

  Or am I dreaming?

My knees are shaking
My mouth is dry
My eyes are moist

  This isn't like me, Lord.
  If anything, I've been
  too casual . . .
  perhaps even arrogant
  about my role as husband.

Why should I worry now?
It's a little too late, isn't it?

  Father in heaven,
  I'll be good to her!

I'll be the man You
expect me to be!
I'll live up to the vows
we'll soon be making
but it's going to take Your help.

It won't be natural to share my time
and worldly goods with someone else.

I've been so independent
I've been so complacent
I've been so noncommittal
about my relationship to You
that I'm not sure I can
be a very good husband.

Wake me up, Lord,
before the ceremony's over!
Please?

The Fading Prince

Lord, he's not what I expected
nor what I really wanted
but thanks to You
I'm satisfied.
And grateful!

I had looked for a Prince Charming
and that's almost what I got.
He was good looking
but lacked character.
He was well educated
but too self-sufficient.

He didn't need You
and he didn't need me, either.

I want to be needed, Lord;
I need to be wanted, too.
That's when I began to look elsewhere.
Successfully (if I may put it that way).

He isn't much to look at
but he has character.
He's not very well educated
but he'll be a steady provider.
He's not a snappy dresser
but he wears well.

Lord, how can I thank You enough
for opening my eyes
before it was too late?

I'm not really excited
but I am content.
I'm not going out of my mind
but I know I have a future.
I'm not madly in love
but the bond between us
is greater than passion or lust.

My only hope, Lord, is that he'll get
half as much as I'm getting . . .

On Learning How to Love

Thanks, Lord, for keeping us apart
before we came together.

She's a sweetheart, only a child,
and if I could
I'd keep her this way
forever.

She's not a great cook, yet,
but soon she'll surpass her mother—
and mine.

It's amazing, Lord, the way
she's turned our little house
into a home.

She's a whiz with the budget
(I never could manage very well)
and keeps me on my toes
(which no one else could manage).

She's incredible with kids
and the elderly love her, too.

She hasn't an enemy in the world
and our neighbors keep beating
a path to our door
    a cup of sugar
    a spot of tea
    an encouraging word
    a bit of advice . . .

But I don't mind sharing her, Lord.
Isn't the name of the game
    sharing
    caring
    daring . . .

Lord, love is eternal.
Couldn't it be longer?

More Than a Roommate

Marriage isn't what I thought.
It's infinitely better!
    Thanks for bringing us together, Lord.

I married a boy
but he's quickly
becoming a man.

I have a new roommate, Lord,
but he's much better than
my dormmate.

I've inherited a big brother, too,
who treats me with such protective love.

I've moved in with a working man
but thanks to automatic washers
and miracle soaps I don't mind.

I'm living with a student and
night classes but this won't
last forever.

I'm married to a first-class
handyman but I really don't
mind sharing him with our neighbors.

I'm in love, Lord, with a lover,
and the sooner I can bear his child,
the better.

I have a companion, Lord, who is
as willing to go my way as
I am his . . .

I have a good provider, too,
and although our lifestyle
is a bit meager, we aren't
suffering one little bit.

Best of all, Lord, I've
married a priest who is
not ashamed to pray.

I did pretty well, didn't I?

Quibbles and Quarrels

Lord, it takes
"two to tangle." I know!
   When I lived alone I was
   bored
   uninspired
   lonely
but I had few quibbles or quarrels.

If the towel was left on the floor
it was I who dropped it there.

If the coffee was too strong
I blamed no one but myself.

   Now we quibble over trivialities
   such as soggy toast and
   quarrel over mundane matters
   such as mismatched socks.

Why, Lord, can't we pull out
all the stops and get it over with?

Must we nag until alimony
shuts us up?!?

Must we fiddle around
while our marriage burns?

   Forgive me, Lord, if I sound upset
   (which I am) but why can't we
   have one big fight and get it
   out of our systems?!?

I'm weary of silly, stupid quarrels
with their uninspired, "I'm sorry, Dear."

   I'm scared, Lord, because I see
   our marriage slowly disintegrating
   when it might be better if it would explode.

37

At least then we could pick up the pieces.
If we could find them.

Lord, please—since we can't
seem to do it—take the whimper
out of our lives.

Shattered Solitude

What a revolting development
I thought it was going to be.
    Imagine!
Inheriting my husband's grandfather
as a permanent houseguest.

At first I was incensed
when we were asked
to make a home for an
old codger who was obviously
living in the twilight zone.

    How selfish I was
    even though it was
    a normal reaction.

    Young marriages need
    solitude, not tenants.

Now he's gone
but his spirit
and wisdom linger on.

Lord, I can close my eyes
and his words ring in my ears:

    "Communicate, honey, communicate"
    "Chip away at the rough edges, my love,
    but don't knock his block off"

"Listen, sweet love, fix what
you like to eat, too"
"Do your own thing, child, but
not all the time"
"Sock it to him, baby, but remember,
no low blows."
I miss him, Lord.
These ten years virtually
guarantee the next forty—
    thanks to an absolutely
    marvelous old codger who had
    never heard of the twilight zone.

Colorblind

Lord, we don't live in a shack
on the Mississippi—
We live in a condominium
overlooking a swimming pool.

    What's happened in the last
    hundred years? Or in the last
    three thousand?

If I remember correctly, Lord,
you were pleased with the Israelites
who accepted the Egyptians
who elected to go with them
from the land of the Nile.

You know, Lord, we aren't black and white
We aren't even red and yellow
If anything, we are copper and bronze
    and copper and bronze is
    beautiful because You
    made it so.

When we dated people stared
When we married people glared

> How long, Lord, must
> we endure this?
> Forever?

Her people merely tolerate me
My people are reservedly polite

> Right now all we have
> is each other. And You.

Lord, must we wait until
the next life when we
will all be colorblind—
> like You?

Chauvinism Crystallized

Before I married him
I thought he was a bit
> self-centered
> chauvinistic
> prejudiced
but I married him anyway.

Before long I realized
that he thought I was
> independent
> chauvinistic
> liberated . . .

Imagine, Lord, we both thought
of each other as chauvinistic—
and we are!

Frankly, Lord, I'll have to admit

that I thought I knew what
chauvinism meant until
one day I looked it up:
   "excessive devotion to a cause"
   "zealous and belligerent patriotism"

Teasingly (but with some acid) one day
I called him a **male chauvinist pig**
and he retaliated by smiling.

That did it, Lord.

   I was fighting for women's rights
   He was fighting for men's rights

   I was fighting with words
   He was fighting with smiles

He won, Lord!
Now we're both fighting
for human rights.

Equal Partnership

You won't believe it, Lord,
but I'm eating those words
I threw at You when we married.

   The taste is awful
   but I'll get over it.

As you remember, I told everyone:
   my bride
   her parents
   my people
   the minister
that we live in the **Twentieth Century**
which calls for a new outlook

on matrimony
(and a few other things) . . .

We agreed to go fifty-fifty
on everything we said and did
(which was an absurd agreement).

   I washed, she ironed
   I shopped, she cooked
   (I cooked, she shopped)
   I washed the car
   She washed the windows

   I made the deposits
   She paid the bills

   She named the artist
   I got the tickets
   She chose the style
   I picked the brand

It worked beautifully
until we discovered impasses
that a vote couldn't settle.

What does one do with a
string of 1-1 verdicts?

   Well, anyway, we took another vote
   Now I'm head of the house
The vote was 0-2 (ladies first!)
Think I can hack it, Lord?

Hot Honeymoons

I suppose You saw the report
which said that couples prefer

hot climates for their honeymoon.
   Sounds logical, doesn't it?
We went South but we didn't have
such a hot honeymoon . . .

   We were ready for the engagement
   We were all set for the wedding
   but we overlooked the honeymoon.

In all the excitement
and dizziness of festivities
we neglected our honeymoon.

Now we know why You made
such a fuss about the first year
of marriage.

Lord, we were rookies
      amateurs
      novices
but we thought we were sophisticated
      experienced
      knowledgeable
      polished . . .

   We fooled no one
   except ourselves

   Lord, climate is important
   but we thought it all-important.

   'A year has gone by now
   and we are doing nicely
   but for our Anniversary
   we're heading North.

We thought this time
we'd try a cooler climate.

No Experience Necessary

My Dear Lord,
I think I'm runnin'
low on fuel. When I do,
I'll just stick my big thumb out
and You can give me a ride Home . . .

After fifty years of
    preaching
    teaching
    marrying
    burying
    counseling
    pushing and maybe even
    shovin' a little,
nothing beats standing in front of
two beautiful young people and
looking deep down into their eyes
as they murmur, **I do.**

We've got the front row seats,
haven't we, Lord? Those out
in the congregation don't know
what they're missin' . . .

    Lord, I've seen everything:
        common-law weddings
        shotgun ceremonies
        repeaters
        manipulators
        con artist festivities
        elopement ratifications
    and you name it . . .

Big weddings with orchestras and
little ones with a harmonica . . .

But Lord, there's never anything
more splendid than uniting
two novices in holy wedlock.

I guess it isn't all bad
not knowing exactly
what lies ahead, is it?

PARENTING

You Don't Love Me Anymore

Lord, O my Lord,
what can I do?

When I come home at night
the house is a total mess—
the kids are screaming
the wife is half-crazy
the supper hasn't had a chance
and . . . well, You know how it is!

There was a time when
I loved her dearly but
that was many pounds and
fewer kids ago.

I say she's disorganized;
She says she's overworked.

I say she feels sorry for herself;
She says I don't love her anymore.

Maybe she's right.

The fire hasn't gone out
but it's getting pretty low.

I say she needs a break
but she won't leave the kids.

Lord, I love these little ones,

indeed I do, but these rascals are
ruining our marriage.

That's not what kids are for, is it?

"Be fruitful, multiply, replenish . . ."
Isn't that what You said?!?

Lord, please touch our marriage.
We may not know it
but we need a miracle.

Nothing short of a miracle
can save us now. Nothing.

I don't know if I believe in miracles, Lord,
but I think I'd recognize one if I saw one.

Security Without a Blanket

I guess, Lord, I wasn't prepared
because I didn't realize that
marriage is
    ecstasy with reservations
    security without a blanket
    comradery with new dimensions
    adjustment without a timetable
    traveling on a one-way ticket
    flying blind much of the time
    falling and getting up again
    saying I'm sorry repeatedly
    arguing heatedly as well as feebly
    making-up with regularity . . .

I never knew that
marriage is
    such hard work
    so much trial and error . . .

Had I known, Lord,
I might have avoided it
or postponed it indefinitely
  but then I would have
  been the loser.

Marriage is growing on us, Lord,
which is good. Otherwise, we'd mature
and ripen much too soon.

  I think this is Your idea
  because marriages should
    bend with the breeze
    weather the storms
    blossom in the sun and
    struggle against
    winds that blow continually.

Already our marriage has moved
from playing house to
building a home.

  Soon, Lord Jesus, we'll want
  someone to share it with us.

Cheaper by the Dozen?

Lord, all my life
I've dreamed about
having a large family.

  Oh, maybe not a dozen
  but at least half . . .

When I tell my friends
or my parents
they rise in unison:

  That's a thing of the past

Ever heard of planned parenthood?
How'll you feed so many?
You're upsetting our ecology
You live in a city, not on a farm
With only one wife?

Lord, isn't this our business?
We agreed before marriage
to have all the children we could afford:
    physically
    mentally
    economically

Now that we have five with
another on the way
we have incurred the wrath
of nearly everyone . . .

Worse than that,
my wife is plagued with doubts,
which has me feeling guilty.
    I thought, Lord, that
    children were **cheaper by the dozen,**
    not parents cheapened by a half!

The Child of Our Choice

I can't believe You
planned it this way, Lord,
but if You did,
please accept our gratitude.
    We love each other
    more dearly than ever
    since we discovered
    we cannot have children.

At first we were confused,
then bitter, but now we're
reconciled to it even though
we realize it may take years
before we can have a child
of our choice.

> When she couldn't conceive,
> I blamed her, then You, then everybody.
> What a fool I was.

We've talked it over
We've prayed about it
We've shed many tears
  bitter tears
  soft sobs and
  even some sniffles

We've considered adopting
  an orphan of another race
  a child who never had a chance
  a babe with a handicap
  an infant who looks like us

Father, we don't want to be
selfish or cruel, unrealistic or heroic
  but we're not sure of either
  our capabilities or our wisdom . . .

Please, Dear Father,
help us make the right choice!

Solidarity

Dear Jesus,
Thank You for Mommie

and Daddy and for Grandma
and Grandpa . . .

I wasn't so good today
so I really don't know
what to say.

Want to know something?
I think my Mommie overreacted,
don't You? After all,
it was an accident and
she can always buy another—uh,
what do you call those things—
chandelier.

What gets me, Jesus,
is why Daddy got so upset.
I really didn't mean to throw the ball
so high but I guess it slipped.

Why do grownups always
stick together? Either one
of them could have handled it,
right?

At least then I'd have
one friend around here.

Well, good-night, Jesus.
It's nice to know
you aren't angry.

See You in the morning.

"To Be or Not To Be"

I'm pregnant again, Lord,
but I can't handle it

54

What went wrong?

We took every precaution
We planned so carefully

Three drove me up a wall
What will four do?

To be brutally honest,
I don't think I can manage it

He wants me to have an abortion
(for my mental well-being)
I'm afraid

No, not of surgery,
but the side effects

Lord, will I suffer remorse?
Will guilt and shame follow me
all the days of my life?

We've always thanked You
for giving us three beautiful children
Do we dare take another away
without asking Your permission?

Lord, why am I troubled?
These aren't Victorian days
Modern medicine is marvelous
and certainly society is affirming

If I ask You for Your approval
I'm afraid I know what You'll say
so I'm not going to ask

But I would like to make
a deal with you

If we keep the baby,
will You promise
never to leave me or forsake me?

A Matter of Time

Measles, whooping cough, influenza,
runny nose, chicken pox, pneumonia,
   broken bones, smashed thumbs,
   chipped teeth, pierced ears,
   rejected term papers, shattered dreams . . .
So far so good.

   But leukemia?
   Why, Lord,
   why???

Had we a dozen
we wouldn't have had
one to spare
   but our only child—
   I don't understand.

Sure, Lord, I believe in miracles
Or, at least I think I do
   She's in remission, we're told,
   but it's only a matter of time.

A matter of time.
I hate that sentence, Lord
   It's cruel
   It's vicious
   It's inhuman

Remember, for ten years we waited
for the child of our hopes and
immediately presented her to You.

   Now, seventeen years later,
   we're expected to part with her.

Oh, Lord, we're not angry with You—
Somehow we get the feeling

that You are extremely upset, too.

We know that in the next world
sickness and death will be vanquished
but, Lord, how we wish it were now.

Ten in a Row

How marvelous these little ones are, Lord
I wouldn't trade them
for all the sunshine in Acapulco
for all the degrees at State
for a Mercedes Benz
or for whatever couples do
in lieu of parenting . . .

Nothing shall separate me
from loving **Awful Andy**—
sure, he's sometimes as mean as sin
but I think our tough love
is beginning to pay off

Who can ignore **Blushing Brenda**?
she's so shy no one thinks
she's related to Andy but let
someone speak evil of her—
ouch, they'll have to reckon with him

And then there's **Cornball Carlos**
what a character: lovable,
demonstrative, demanding, but
a heart of pure gold

Ah, if I had a favorite (but I don't) . . .
How grateful we are for **Dancing Denise**
I swear, Lord, she wears out
a pair of shoes every week—

she never walks or runs,
only dances because she's so happy

Do, Lord, remember **Eddie, the Engineer**
Nothing, I mean nothing,
stays together around here
when he's around. But one of these days,
he'll learn to put things
back together again. Won't he?

Ten in a Row (continued)

Thank You, kind Jesus, for **Finicky Flora**
She's so precious. Oh, if I'd
let her, she'd bother me plenty,
but we let her eat when she wants
and wear what she's got

Tell me, Lord, how'd we get one
like **Gruesome George?**
He's cute, he is. Someday—
You watch and see—he'll be
well-coordinated and handsome.
Until then, please give me just
a little bit more love for the child.
And more tolerance for those mean ones
who gave him the nickname

Heavenly Helene
is a marvelous child, Lord.
So sensitive in spiritual matters,
so dedicated to You, and so influential
on the rest of us

Lordy me, if I'll ever understand
Intellectual Ivan . . .
studies come so easily but

he helps the younger, and
the older, if they'll let him

Finally, Lord, do bless **Jealous Julie**—
she'll outgrow it I'm sure
but meanwhile, thank You for her
warm personality and willing hands . . .

Yes, Jesus, You've given
us a wonderful family.
People do stop and stare sometimes
but we don't mind. In fact, we're
proud, grateful, and usually broke
but we can hardly wait until we're
grandparents.

Then we'll parent by proxy.
Praise the Lord!

Once Is Enough

Lord, Adam and Eve
didn't have much to go on,
did they?

Is that why Cain
clobbered his brother?
No, I can't believe that.
Adam and Eve weren't perfect, but who is?

Why did You entrust such an important
task to novices? Parenting
is such an exacting profession . . .

This bothered me, Lord,
until I considered the alternatives:
baby farms
genetic control
selective parenting

controlled environments
immaculate nurseries
insulated dormitories
graded curricula
visitation regulations . . .

Forbid it, Lord.
No wonder You chose
rookies to be parents.

And rookies we are.

Just when we think we've mastered the trade
we're confronted with a brand new problem

Maybe that isn't all bad
since it keeps us on our toes.

I don't know what Adam and Eve did
when Abel didn't come home that night
but I have a hunch . . .

Thank You, Lord, for trusting novices
with the pain and pleasure of parenthood.
You're right, too. Once is enough!

The Day I Rose from the Dead

Yesterday I was ready to
write You off—
today I'm ashamed . . .

Everyone was so kind—
In fact, I suppose we were
killed with kindness.

Never have I gone through
such a battle with my emotions:
I grieved
I wept and I fought the tears

I despaired
I blamed You and myself
I died

I really did, Lord.
I died and rose again.

I know, Lord, that You knew
she was only six months
when You took her . . .

Over and over I screamed,
   You took her!
   You took her!
   You took her!

I didn't give her to You, Lord
   She didn't have an incurable disease
   She didn't have a lingering illness

   She died of complications
   following a simple cold
   which turned into pneumonia
   attacking weaknesses
   we never knew she had.

Lord, now I know that You knew best.

She's Yours, Dear Lord.
Please take good care of her.
If You think it possible,
dare we ask for another?

Don't Feel Sorry for Us

Why, Lord, do people
feel so sorry for us?

I think I understand in part
because at first I was

bewildered
disgusted
discouraged
frustrated
but it didn't last long.

Before we knew it, this little one
grabbed our hearts and
never let go!

Usually I don't weep, Lord,
but today I couldn't help it.
Some woman whispered behind my back:
**Oh, my God, how could anyone
handle a hideous child like that?**

I don't think she was talking to You,
nor do I think she realized what she said.

We love our little imperfect one
more than words can tell. Maybe this
deformity has given us more love,
patience, tenderness, understanding . . .
I really don't know.

What we do know is this:
We love him dearly
We love You more than ever
And never have we known more love
for each other.

Can You imagine that people
feel sorry for us?

Three Under Five

Lord, I've often wondered
why You scolded Your disciples
for keeping the little ones

from climbing all over You.
Now I know!

With three under five
I've been called everything:
cruel
inconsiderate
chauvinistic
unpatriotic
inhuman

I've taken more slams
than a back door:
Got stock in a diaper company?
Ever hear of planned parenthood?
Raisin' yer own kindergarten?
Tryin' to cheat Uncle Sam?
Sleepin' off yer frustrations?

Lord, I suppose I ought to fight back
or be bitter or something but I'm not.

Sometimes, when I close my eyes,
I can see You with all those little
kids climbing up into Your lap.

A great feeling, isn't it?

Lord, I feel sorry for the man
who never trips over a rollerskate . . .
who never walks the floor at night . . .
who never gets a slobbery kiss at 5:00 a.m.

Since You, Jesus, loved kids
but never had any of Your own,
I'd be honored if You'd consider
our kids Your kids, too.

This would help take the sting
out of some of these stingers.

Give Me a Son, or Else!

Lord, when I discovered
I was to be a mother
I literally jumped for joy.

My happiness was short-lived.

My husband made it
as clear as he knew how:
"Give me a son, or else!"

At first I thought he was teasing
and I responded accordingly.

Now I know he is dead serious.

Everything he does involves a son.
I'm barely one-third along the way
and our "son" has a room full of toys:
a football and a baseball mitt
a firetruck and a police car
a wardrobe of boys clothing
and he even papered the room
accordingly.

At first it was a desire
but it has become an obsession
and I don't know how to handle it.

I'm frightened, Lord, I really am.
Today when I gently suggested that
it might be a girl
he nearly went berserk.

He won't listen to me
He won't listen to our pastor
He won't listen to reason

Lord, I'd ask You—
I'd even beg—

for a son if I dared . . .

Right now, You are all I have.
If You can't get through to him,
no one can.

One Is Too Many

Why we didn't talk it over
before we were married
I do not know.

All I know is that
we made a mistake.

I love children
and I thought he did
He was always so kind to children
He seemed to have so much patience
He actually fussed over babies
which led me to believe
without asking
that he wanted some of his own
someday.

How wrong I was
How stubborn he is

I suppose I could **accidently**
have a child
but I think that would
destroy our marriage . . .

I suppose I could acquiesce
to his will
but that would eventually
destroy our marriage, too.

As I see it,
no matter what I do
I lose and if I lose
we both lose.

Lord, I feel shame, guilt, and remorse
for not settling this before
but really, how was I to know?

Lord, maybe time is what we both need.
If so, I'll need more patience and love.

I hope You have a little of each to spare.

Electronic Babysitters

Ever since I resumed my career
we've never had it so good—
or bad.

Financially, we're ahead.
Family-wise, we're behind.

I was a good mother, Lord.
I laid out a snack for the kids
to nibble on when they came home from
school and made sure the TV sets were functioning.

We trusted our youngsters
and they never betrayed this trust.

Slowly it dawned on me.
I was barely noticed when I came home.
I seldom heard what had happened in school.
I dared not interrupt either
program or commercial.

Dinner seemed to be an intrusion

on their private world and more and more
we ate by TV.

In short, Lord, I had been
replaced by a gadget.

Lord, I've often wondered what you think
of working wives. Personally, I love
getting out and keeping my career alive.
I am more efficient and the time I have
with the kids has more quality
even if less quantity . . .

You've heard that before, haven't You?

When I think of them, I feel guilty
When I think of me, I feel content
When I think of You, I don't know
how I feel . . .

Lord, do You expect more of me
than I do?

ESTRANGEMENT

Estranged?

My Lord and my God,
if I could only know
what estrangement is . . .

> For years we have been married
> but I have never known love.

> Unwisely, I married to save face
> and he married me for basically
> the same reason.

We went through all the motions
We developed an aura of respectability
We behaved as decent parents
We fooled scores of people
> but we never fooled ourselves
> and I know we haven't fooled You.

> Now we maintain a house
> and provide a shelter
> for our children
> but no more . . .

We are civil, polite, cautious
We are respected, admired, envied

> That's the tragedy, Lord
> We are actually envied
> (if people only knew)

I have never been loved—
I have never known contentment
and I'm afraid the same
is true for my bitter half . . .

Oh, if I knew love—
I would understand estrangement
and could do something about it.

As it is, Lord, we haven't
grown apart. We were never
together. Ours is the union
of a robot with a mannequin,
living in a doll house,
playing games.

Father, Forgive Them . . .

"Father, forgive them
for they know not what they do."

How could You pray that way?
After what they had done to You?

Lord, I can't forgive them
I won't forgive them
I've tried—oh, how I've tried
but I can't try any longer.

Everything I do is wrong
Everything I say is distorted
Everything I cook is snubbed
Every place I go is questioned
Every friend I have is suspect
Every dollar I spend is wasted

I'm a poor mother,

a bad housekeeper,
and an even worse driver.

Yesterday I refused to talk
on the phone to my mother-in-law.
Today I slammed the door in her face!
Tomorrow . . .

Tomorrow!!! I'm worried, Lord.
I don't know what I'll do.
That's why I had to talk to You.

If she comes again,
maybe You'd better answer the door.

Venom and Honey

In-laws!

When You thought of marriage,
did You overlook in-laws?

I suppose You might have had
something else in mind because
we do not live under the roof of
either set of parents nowadays.

Even so, marriage is designed
for all cultures and lifestyles,
isn't it?

Lord, I need some help . . .

Her parents kill us with kindness—
My parents murder us with meanness.
This constant diet of
venom and honey is
deadly.

Her parents think I'm a jewel

Mine believe I married a fool

Her parents can't do enough for us
Mine continually plot against us

I suppose these ought to be offsetting
but it doesn't work that way.

Her parents always pick up the tab
Her in-laws usually send a bill.

My in-laws anticipate our needs
My parents hope we find out the hard way.

What more could we want?
What more can we say?

One set shoves us off the deep end
and the other comes to the rescue.

What can we do, Lord?
We love them both but
our love seems to be wearing thin—
for them—
and between the two of us.
Should we surrender, or fight?

Three Times and Out

This is the last time, Lord,
I swear it is!

Wedding bells are ringing again
and I don't know who I am or
where I'm going.

Never, Lord, never again
will I question Your wisdom.

Once is enough!

I did some tallying—

now I know why I'm going crazy

> Three kids from marriage number one
> One from number two (ours) and
> two from his previous marriage . . .
> None (of ours) from number three
> but four (all grown) from his.
> Confused?

Do You know what this means, Lord?

> Four are my flesh and blood
> Six are by adoption—of sorts

> Ten children, six parents
> (plus two more from their divorces),
> seventeen grandchildren and
> in-laws all over the place.

Suzie (I mean Susan)
wants her real father
to walk her down the aisle
but her stepfather
resents it bitterly
("Eighteen years I've given that kid
and look what she does to me," he says).

> As I look back over the years,
> none of my marriages were that bad—
> or good. The first could have been
> as good as the others
> had I hung in there.

Help me, Lord, lest I get hung again.

Cozy While It Lasted

I never did give much thought
to why we never married.

Probably for the same reason
I never gave You much thought.

　I thought I was in control
　I didn't need or want You
　I thought it couldn't happen to me

But it did!

We did pretty well for a few years
but I guess the enchantment wore off.
I suppose, Lord, we behaved like
so many married folks—we simply
took each other for granted.

When he walked out
I had nothing. In fact,
he never told me . . .
he simply took his belongings
and disappeared.

　I got the apartment
　with all the bills.

　I got the children
　with all their ills.

Well, it was cozy while it lasted.

You know, Lord, how I reacted:

　I was hurt and angry
　I thought of suing
　I considered suicide

Then I came to my senses
and thought of You. Lord,
if You only knew how embarrassed
I was . . . I almost didn't
call Your name . . .

He's gone, Lord. For good—

because I'll never take him back.

You'll forgive me for
saying *never,* won't you?

When the Light Grows Dim

I'm listening, Lord . . .

Why didn't anyone tell us
that passion fades?

I didn't think about it then
but I sure do now.
When I think of our honeymoon
and our first child . . .
We were high then, Lord, and
I mean high.
Now we can't get it back . . .

We're trying hard
to make an adjustment
but we're not succeeding too well

Little things irritate us
Bills keep piling up
Sex isn't as important
The house looks tacky
The yard is a mess
Short nights and colic
are taking their toll . . .

I read somewhere that passion
in a marriage seldom lasts
five years—often less.
I didn't want to believe it
but I'm a believer now.

Where do we go from here?
    If passion and interest fade
    and problems and tensions mount,
    what did You have in mind
    to keep a marriage going?

What's that, Lord?

You are suggesting
that we become friends—
to develop a friendship?

    That's too simple, isn't it?

A Rude Awakening

Slowly I'm getting over my anger
toward You for taking Bill away from me.

    Twelve years wasn't enough
    but it was enough to show me
    how much I took him for granted.

Why is it, Lord,
that death is such
a rude awakening
for those of us
who live on?

    I miss him more now
    that he's gone than I
    appreciated him
    when he was alive.

    Especially with the children.

I'm high-strung, aggressive,
quick-tempered, sometimes mean,
but he was easy-going, considerate,

without a mean bone in his body.

He had such a calming effect
on the kids—and me.

Why couldn't I see it then?
Why did I nag
scold
criticize and
push until I nearly
destroyed him?

Bill complemented me, Lord
He covered a multitude of my sins
He made life more than bearable

Why You let him get away I don't know
but please tell him we miss him—terribly!
More than he could possibly have imagined.

Equal Time

Lord, we had the perfect arrangement!
we agreed to share
the children equally.
On paper it was ideal . . .

None of the weekend only stuff
None of the holiday rigamarole
None of the brutal bribery bit

No Sir, Lord. Not for us!
If we couldn't handle our affairs
at least we could keep our children
from being destroyed in the process.

We alternated custody
every ninety days

reversing the process
every two years . . .

For a while it worked well
until Easter fell in March
one year and in April the next
causing me to miss out
on both holidays.

You know, Lord, that this was
only an excuse for suing for
complete custody. Our **perfect**
system was imperfect because
we are imperfect:

we did compete with each other
we did subtly bribe our children
we did belittle each other
we did harbor grudges
we did play games
we did miss each other
we did long for former friends
we did feel guilt and shame
we did date with mixed motives . . .

Yes, Lord, I won custody
of the little ones but my problems
are not solved. Not completely.

Perhaps, Lord, I should have sued
for custody of my ex-husband.

Extramarital Vows

Oh, Lord, I'm getting weary.
Maybe it's my age

but I think not.

One of the vows I made
was to dominate our marriage
and that I have done

Economically
Socially
Religiously
Vocationally

I built him up
and cut him down

I tugged and pushed
and bent him out of shape

I belittled and praised,
manipulated and schemed

I whined and screamed
and even resorted to forms
of blackmail and extortion

Now, after all these years,
I've whittled him into the shape he's in
and so I'm stuck with
my kind of man

I tampered with his ego
I destroyed his personality
I shattered his self-esteem

Lord, I have no desire or strength
to remake my man even if I could

Pardon the expression, but
I've made my bed and now
I must sleep in it.

Alone. He'll have no part of me.

Ill-Conceived

Oh, Lord, I'm bewildered
    baffled
    bitter, and now
    banished . . .

I know, Lord, You know the reason
lies elsewhere but that doesn't
seem to be terribly consoling.

Once again the doctor
tried to explain the inexplicable—
he refuses to listen.

Why, Lord, did You
make him incapable
instead of me?

  It would have been so much easier.

I can accept it
but he can't—or won't.

He still blames me, Lord,
and now he wants an
annulment . . .

  He thinks I deceived him
  and so he **wants out** . . .

I ought to hate him but I can't
I ought to pity him but I don't
I ought to let him go but I won't

Just how long I can go on
living this way pretty much
depends on You rather than me
because I just don't have much left
except a stubborn will . . .

  Yes, Lord, I have considered divorce

and other alternatives but none of
them are solutions.

Lord, can You touch his eyes
to make him see? Or better yet,
touch his body and set him free?

RECONCILIATION

In-Laws or Outlaws?

Thank You, Lord,
for giving me such marvelous in-laws

> Our marriage (as You know)
> was losing its luster
> and, frankly, I guess it was
> impossible to hide.

Mom sensed that not all was well
and discreetly told me a
few helpful things
about her "little boy."

> What a revelation
> What a revolution

I should have known some
of his idiosyncrasies
before we were married
(but then I might not
have married him) . . .
I should have sensed some of
his needs but never gave them
much thought . . .

> She reminded me that
> he is sanguine, not choleric
> (I had been pushing too hard)

She reminded me that
he is sensitive, not callous
(I was trying to make him tough)

She reminded me that he needed a wife
(I was trying to mother him)

Lord, what a change in our marriage
And in me!

Easy Over

I hate men.
I hate them all!

Big ones, little ones,
old, young, fat, skinny,
rich, poor, smart, stupid,
married or single . . .

I hate 'em!

We were eating breakfast
so I asked him how
he wanted his eggs.

"Easy over."

Of course I knew before I asked
but I guess I wasn't paying
too much attention
and roughed them up a bit.

"You call that easy over?"

He didn't have to scream at me
but I suppose I didn't have to
yell back, either.

Anyway, Lord, he left the table,

dumped the eggs in the garbage
and stomped out the door.
Wow, what a baby.

Was I angry?
I'm still fuming.

Tonight I'm going to burn everything—
the meat, potatoes, carrots, pie.
I'll even burn the coffee!

Oh, excuse me, Lord.
Someone's at the door.

Guess what? A dozen roses with two words:
"I'm sorry!" Whoopie!

No burnt offering tonight.

Too Many Opinions

As You know, Lord,
our marriage is in trouble.
I'm sorry, but that's how it is.

Our friends know it
Our kids know it
Our parents know it
Our neighbors suspect it

If anything, Lord,
we're getting too much advice

Our friends say go to a counselor
Our kids say we need a vacation
Our parents suggest a psychiatrist
Our neighbors aren't talking (to us)

We've tried it all

counseling (clinics and therapy)
vacationing (together and separately)
psychiatry (one at a time)

Now we're so confused
we don't know who we are
or what we're doing.

Lord, we don't want to call it quits
but we can't continue this way

In desperation I went to our pastor
He was sympathetic, kind, understanding
but said nothing about clinical counseling
or psychiatry. He simply said when we're
through talking to everyone to come back.

Do You suppose
he knows what he's
talking about?

Bone China and Caribbean Cruises

Why can't I tell her, Lord?

When I grew up
my mother and father
used gushy, endearing terms
they never meant:
darling
sweetheart
dearest
honey . . .

If anything, they despised
each other.

To this day, Lord, I cannot
call my wife **darling** or **sweetheart.**

I've tried but it sounds hollow

and never seems to come out right.

Even so, I know she's not satisfied with
   roses
   chocolates
   bone china and
   Caribbean cruises.

How do I tell her I love her
when words strangle my feelings?

How can we talk of love
when she won't let me show her?

   Lord, my roses and chocolates
   are neither alms nor bribes—
   they are words put into deeds.

Why is it, dear Lord, that I
can talk so easily with You?

Maybe I should tell You—aloud—
how I feel and hope she overhears.

   You wouldn't mind,
   would You?

Smashing!!!

How does one say "I'm sorry"
through clenched teeth?

It got so I couldn't stand the sight of her:
   everything she did irked me
   everything she said annoyed me
   everything we did bored me

Naturally, it was her fault

   Sure, I knew I had faults
   but I was so much better than she.
   In fact, I didn't realize

how jaundiced I really was.
It was terrible!

Actually, Lord, I began to believe it:
   I was smart, she was stupid
   I was handsome, she was ugly
   I was attractive, she was repulsive
   I was righteous, she was unrighteous
   I was sophisticated, she was uncultured
   I was going places, she wasn't.
   It was unbelievable!

Thanks to Your hammer, I'm softening:
   I'm easier to live with
   I'm more gentle with the kids
   I'm less dictatorial and
   I'm even going to a counselor.

Lord, I hate myself this way
   I want to say I'm sorry but I won't
   I want to be forgiven but I can't
Not until I'm broken.

Lord, what comes first:
   a broken bottle
   or a smashed spirit?
Or is it a broken spirit
and a smashed bottle?

Whatever, Lord, You do it—
I can't!

Thirty-seven Long Years

Thirty-seven years, Lord,
and he wants to call it quits.
Doesn't he realize it's been
equally long for me?

Maybe even longer . . .

I pressed him, Lord
I pressed him hard
"Why," I asked,
"why now?"

His chances of remarrying
are better—much better—
than mine (if that's what he wants).

Do You know what his answer was?
Most profound: "I'm tired."

Tired.
Imagine.

So I asked him,
"Tired of what?"

"Not what," he says,
"who!"

Then it hit me, Lord.
He wasn't tired of marriage.
He was tired of me.

I couldn't fight it.

I knew I couldn't fight
a dying marriage but
I knew I could fix
a sagging me.

That's when things began to change.

Now we're working on thirty-eight
with great plans for our fortieth!

Forty-nine and Going Strong

Our neighbors almost called it quits
after only thirty-seven years.

We can hardly wait until our fiftieth.

> Oh, she gets a bit ornery
> now and then, Lord,
> but then,
> I'm a stubborn ol' cuss, too.

We tried to be neighborly
to those two but they told us
to mind our own business
and I hardly blame them
(but when you've got something
good going you sort of like
to pass it along) . . .

> When the going gets rough
> we both get out and push.

> When the going is good
> we both enjoy the ride.

In the morning she is
happy to see me go—
when evening rolls around
she is glad to see me again.

> We never talk much about it
> but somehow she knows her job
> and I know mine—
> and we do 'em.

Lord, as the kids say,
she doesn't **send me** anymore
but then, I don't **send her,** either.
Even so, I could no more part with her
than I could part with You.

> Maybe that's why we're
> still going strong,
> 'eh?

Grand Central Station

Lord, we've got to do something—
We can't go on like this.

We are all too busy
The TV is too noisy
Little League is a rat race
School isn't school any more:
    band and orchestra
    year books and newspapers
    rocking chair marathons
    field trips and parties
    driver's ed
    volleyball and baseball
    tennis and golf
    hardly any homework . . .

Church is getting the same:
    Sunday school and worship
    cherub and youth choirs
    drama productions
    Bible camps and retreats
    workathons and car washes
    potlucks and banquets
    nursery duty and cradleroll
    work bees and hobby courses
    Bible studies and committees
    and on and on and on . . .

No, Lord, I'm not really complaining—
Most of it is pretty good
and some of it is necessary—
maybe even vital.

But, Lord, we never see each other
except on the run . . .

Our home is no longer our castle—
It has become Grand Central Station.

We're drifting apart, Lord, and
I don't like it.

Please, Lord, may we have our
cozy little cottage back?

Count Your Blessings

How do I count blessings, Lord,
when I can barely function?
Where do I begin?
   An empty house screaming at me
   A leftover car in the garage
   A nearly full refrigerator
   Beds neatly made
   No more half-empty pop bottles
   Souring milk
   Brown bananas
   A phone which never rings. . . .

For years, Lord, I prayed
for the moment when the kids
would be grown and gone.

   Why didn't someone warn me?

I know I can't have them back
and I suppose deep down
I don't want that
but, Lord, how lonely it is.

I never realized the long hours
he worked to keep things going
and I suppose he won't slow down now—
not merely because I'm lonely . . .

Please, dear Lord,
help me find something
constructive to do.
I suppose I thought I'd
be spending my time
counting my blessings,
but now my blessings
have moved on . . .

For years I've spent my time
loving and being loved
nagging and bragging
praying and paying
    and it's gotten into my blood.
    Don't take it from me, Lord.
    Just let me keep on sharing it.
    With him!

AN ANNOTATED BIBLIOGRAPHY

I have attempted to select books for further reading according to the divisions of this book: **Courtship, Marriage, Parenting, Estrangement** and **Reconciliation.** I have not limited this bibliography to religious works. This may be a gamble but it is a carefully calculated one. It is not an attempt to be all things to all people. In certain "secular" books there are some excellencies that the believer ought not overlook. I would like, however, to make this one cautionary statement: you, and you alone, must separate the wheat from the chaff, the goats from the sheep. Although the typical humanistic approach assumes that sex out of wedlock is not necessarily bad (evil or sinful), and may even imply or state that sexual intercourse is merely another of the many human biological functions that need gratification, the Christian perceives it differently. Even so, there are differing schools of Christian thought and this further muddies the waters.

If you are serious enough to want to dig deeper, the following tools will help you get started. For more resources check the references and bibliographies in these (and other) books, browse in your favorite bookstores (you'll be amazed at the plethora of materials flooding the marketplace), and don't neglect questioning experts in family affairs.

COURTSHIP

Charlie W. Shedd has penned several helpful books on dating. Take a good look at **Letters to Karen** and **Letters to Philip.** If sex is considered a right or a must during courtship, it can hardly become a marriage sacrament. For a general anthology of short articles, you may want to check into **The Marriage Affair,** compiled by J. Allan Petersen. The contributors range from Ann Landers to John R. Rice, and there should be something for everyone. In courtship it is extremely important to understand the unique roles of man and woman. Anything written by Tim and/or Beverly LaHaye will steer you in the direction of understanding individual temperaments and how they affect relationships. David A. Thompson has published **A Premarital Guide For Couples,** which is a questionnaire designed for pastors and counselors. It can be used by couples as well.

MARRIAGE

You should explore clinical studies such as **Human Sexual Response** by William H. Masters and Virginia E. Johnson, **Sexual Loving** by Joseph and Lois Bird and **The Intimate Marriage** by Howard and Charlotte Clinebell. The latter are less clinically oriented but important studies. Because these books are not written from a Christian point of view, they must be read with critical discretion. There is too much good material in these studies to simply ignore them, but their humanistic approach is both subtle and not so subtle.

From a Christian perspective, Dr. Ed Wheat provides a commendable service with his cassettes on "Sex Problems and Sex Technique in Marriage" as well as the book coauthored with his wife, **Intended for Pleasure;** and the LaHaye's popular book, **The Act of Marriage,** has been widely used. There is a must, however: **Solomon on Sex** by Joseph C. Dillow. This is a fascinating interpretation of the Song of Solomon as well as a guide to married love—a practical and devotional book.

PARENTING

Again, an older, secular book should not be overlooked, not as much for its psychology as its common sense, readability and practical insight: **Parents on the Run** by Marguerite and Willard Beecher. Along the same line is James C. Dobson's **Dare to Discipline** (over one million copies sold). Together with his other books, cassettes and films, Dobson must be reckoned with. A line should be given to Paul D. Meier's **Christian Child-Rearing and Personality Development,** which is a reference book aimed at parents and teachers, counselors and clergy. A glance at the footnotes and bibliographies of these and other books will give you additional insights. For a comprehensive, annotated catalogue, write Family Life Publications, Inc., Box 427, Saluda, NC 28773.

ESTRANGEMENT

Divorce, desertion, disillusionment, disgust and disengagement are far too common. Where does one go for help? Dwight Small wrestles with the problem of remarriage in **The Right to Remarry,** as does Helen K. Hosier in **The Other Side of Divorce.** Browse through the shelves of a Christian bookstore and look for names such as Adams, Chandler, Christenson, MacDonald, Mace, Ortlund, Petersen, Taylor, Tournier, Trobish and Wright. Check other bookstores for titles such as **The Intimate Enemy, Parents Without Partners** and **The Two-Paycheck Marriage.** These will assist you in your search.

RECONCILIATION

Just as shipwrecks can be salvaged, individual lives and marriages can be saved, even when all hope seems gone. Here is a partial list of agencies designed to help couples reconcile their differences: Association of Couples for Marriage Enrichment, Inc., P.O. Box 10596, Winston-Salem, NC 27108; Christian Family Movement, 1655 Jackson Boulevard, Chicago, IL 60612; Family Service Association of America, 44 East Twenty-third Street, New York, NY 10010; National Marriage Encounter, 955 Lake Drive, St. Paul, MN 55120; Christian Marriage Enrichment, 8000 E. Girard, Denver, CO 80231; National YMCA, Family Communication Skills Center, 350 Sharon Park Drive, A-23, Menlo Park, CA 94025. Since many of the previously mentioned titles and authors are applicable here as well, let me simply mention a few more titles: **Meet Me in the Middle** by Charlotte H. Clinebell; **Creative Marriage: The Middle Years** by Clayton D. Barbeau and **Alternative to Divorce** by James R. Hine.

As you have noticed, we are not without resources. There are seminars, questionnaires, agencies, periodicals, books, cassettes and movies at our disposal. What may be helpful to one couple may not be to another. Read, study, pray, ask questions and, above all, don't forget that marriage can be more than you dreamed possible.